Powerful Principles

for

Presenters

Powerful Principles

for

Presenters

*Tips for Public Speakers Using
Proven Communication Techniques from
Commercials, Television, and Film Professionals*

Batt Johnson

Writer's Showcase presented by *Writer's Digest*
San Jose New York Lincoln Shanghai

Powerful Principles for Presenters
Tips for Public Speakers Using Proven Communication Techniques from
Commercials, Television, and Film Professionals

Published by Writer's Showcase presented by *Writer's Digest*
an imprint of iUniverse.com, Inc.

For information address:
iUniverse.com, Inc.
620 North 48th Street
Suite 201
Lincoln, NE 68504-3467
www.iuniverse.com

ISBN: 0-595-09362-0

Printed in the United States of America

- A Quick Read
- Easy Guidelines
- Over *300* Insider Tips

Readers Speak About
Powerful Principles for Presenters

"The style of Batt Johnson's book makes me feel that I am working directly with a coach. When I heeded his advice, my public presentations improved. It's a book I will refer to often." **Dr. Carol Robbins-Director, Off-Campus College, Cornell University**

"The next best thing to learning from Batt Johnson in person is what you've got in your hands. He's a master communicator, and this is a great guide to his technique." **Lisa Napoli-Internet Correspondent, MSNBC-TV**

"This book is an exhaustive how-to guide which will provide a primer for the rookie and an effective refresher for the seasoned veteran." **Rapheal M. Prevot Jr.-Labor Relations Counsel, National Football League**

"This comprehensive tome is the 'one-stop-shopping, all-inclusive tour' of everything you needed to know in turning the challenge of public speaking into the opportunity of unleashing the power of communication. As a financial professional, the tips have proved invaluable in the art of 'friendly persuasion.'" **John Krysko-Financial Planner, American Express Co.**

"Thoughtful, insightful, and inspirational! *Powerful Principles for Presenters* offers instruction on the execution of many things you always wanted to do but were afraid to do. This timely workbook is a must-read for anyone who wants to improve their presentation skills. It provides a step-by-step guide for success." **Renee L. Harris-Associate Director, Marketing & Management Institute-New York University**

"All the busy businessperson needs to make presentations with impact is here in Batt Johnson's book. Use the tips from a new chapter before each presentation and watch your success grow. You owe it to your audience to read and use this book!" **Nancy Rosanoff-Past President, National Speakers Association and author of *Making Money Through Intuition***

"If you're interested in a practical, no-nonsense guide to communication, this is the book to read. Batt Johnson's unique insights and techniques have helped me become even more successful as a professional speaker." **Pamela Harper-President, Business Advancement Inc.**

"People who present are always looking for ways to improve. With every aspect of life moving at an accelerated pace—there is often little time for training. *Power Principles for Presenters* is an effective solution." **Chryssa Chin-Professional Sports Executive**

"Batt Johnson's insight, intellect, and experience helped him create a very user-friendly and complete text of tips. Some of these concepts I have never seen or heard of before." **Terrie M. Williams-President/CEO, The Terrie Williams Agency and author of *The Personal Touch***

"As a director, I am constantly speaking at all levels, from staff meetings to formal presentations. Batt Johnson's concise, cut-to-the-chase instructions have provided me with a clear pathway to improving how I communicate everyday. After just four months of applying his instructions, I have seen measurable performance improvements." **D. Scott Harper-Ph.D Section Director, Warner Lambert Company**

"Everyone's apprehensive when called to speak in public, having stage jitters to stage fright. Whether a beginner or professional speaker, Batt Johnson's interactive book will help you personalize the craft of public communication. If your goal is to entertain, educate, and inspire, just apply these exercises and your presentation skills will soar." **Quincy McCoy-author of *No Static: A Guide to Creative Radio Programming***

"*Powerful Principles for Presenters* should be added to the library of any executive, business manager, business owner—anyone who needs to communicate on any level with any other single human being during the course of a day's work. It all starts with the right mental attitude toward public speaking and presentations, and Batt Johnson gives many attainable tips that *work!*" **Nina Kaufman-Counselor at Law, Paltrowitz & Kaufman, New York**

"Batt Johnson's book is direct, easy to read, and useful. I recommend it to others regularly and use it myself." **Mary Ann Allison-Chairman and Chief Cybernetics Officer, Allison~LoBue Group and author of *The Complexity Advantage***

"These techniques helped me overcome the fear of my first live TV broadcast and gave me confidence for a successful and enjoyable experience. I attribute its success to Batt Johnson and his knowledge. The tip sections are filled with many commonsense issues, some I would have never thought of without him." **Lisa L. Parisi, CFA-Managing Director, Valenzuela Capital Partners LLC**

"Batt Johnson's book is great reference material. A glance through it before all presentations is a must!" **Catherine Gale-Manager, Irish Tourist Board**

About Powerful Principles for Presenters

Powerful Principles for Presenters is the textbook used at New York University and Cornell University in Batt Johnson's public speaking classes. It features proven communication techniques from commercials, television, and film professionals and explains their effective use for anyone. This helps you lose any self-consciousness, gain confidence, and deliver your message with as much power as politicians, actors, broadcasters, high profile business executives, and other public speakers seen in the media. When you can speak well you make your points clearly and effectively, convince and motivate others to action, and gain the competitive edge. This information is offered for the first time in one easy-to-read reference book for busy individuals without time to read a large volume the day before an important speech or presentation. This book is interactive-it identifies common problems for public speakers and offers immediate solutions. Each chapter has a workbook section to help you improve your skills, identify action steps, and measure your results.

When you apply these simple, proven tips and techniques you will become a more powerful communicator delivering speeches that roar.

Dedication

My wife, Lisa Aldisert, inspires me in some way everyday. She is a brilliant executive, professional speaker, author, and motivated thinker who gave me the original idea for this book. Because of her insights and inspiration, I have discovered much of the world and a lot more about myself.

She is a gift to the universe, a laser of light and hope, and is always there with a positive contribution in those dark moments of indecision and confusion.

This book represents an intense labor of love to which I dedicate to you, Lisa.

Acknowledgments

I thank the following people for their contribution to the development of this manuscript. The Honorable R. J. Aldisert, whose precise, surgeon-like editing greatly strengthened the manuscript. Paula Dorf for your well-researched tips on makeup for television. Martha Jewett for your guidance on the original manuscript for the business professional. Michael Bernhaut for your friendship and bottomless pit of creative ideas and energy. Johnetta Lever-Ruff for your depth of knowledge of wardrobe and color. Alan Lefkowitz for your continued therapeutic care of the human spirit. Quincy McCoy for your friendship, support, and encouragement to write. Sylvia L. Weber for your editing assistance on the original manuscript. Laura Poole for your editing on the final manuscript. Harley Jane Kozak for your acting memorization tips. Belinda Plutz for your career guidance. Barbara Picard for your transcriptions of my many interviews. For insightful contributions I thank Meredith I. Gertler, James J. Larkin, Alfred A. Lauricella, Alethea B. Lodge-Clarke, Liliana Marchica, Genevieve McMaster, and Ilene Pendrick, the first to use this book in my public speaking class at New York University's Institute of Marketing and Management.

Contents

Section I:
Your Mindset

Chapter 1: Communication:
What is it?

Communication is defined as the process by which individuals give and receive signals that have a specific meaning attached to them. It allows us to share awareness. If one person has knowledge but does not completely or effectively deliver that information to the other person or persons, there is no communication.

The meaning of information can be conveyed orally by altering the tone, intonation, and volume or silently using body language, facial expressions, and gestures. The success of the persuasion, a common goal of communication, also depends on effective use of these elements. Communication can be visual, as in art or a dress code that gives the observer signals, cues or clues to which to react.

The act of communication is not always two-way with a willing giver and receiver. One can easily communicate information without even knowing it. In those instances, the communication is one-way. The art of communication is not merely talking to someone-it is to make that someone your **listener**. Once they are your listener, then you must persuade them.

Tips

The listener must:
- *hear* what is being said.
- *be receptive* to hearing the information.
- *understand* what is being said.
- *attempt* to reciprocate verbally.

The speaker must:
- *speak* as if you know the listener.
- *become* a good listener.

Follow-up

Improvements I Can Make in This Area:

_____

_____

_____

_____

_____

_____

_____

_____

Action Steps to Take:

_____

_____

_____

_____

_____

_____

_____

_____

Results of Action Steps Taken:

_____

_____

_____

_____

_____

_____

_____

Chapter 2: You Are What You Think:
You Will Become What You Wish

Your attitude about what you do makes the difference between a champion and an also-ran. When your sights are set on a specific goal, you unconsciously and consciously move in the direction of your goal. If you **think** you can provide a compelling performance in front of an audience, microphone, or television camera, you will do so. Thinking about it is only half the battle.

You are what you think. You will become what you wish. If you spend time thinking about what will happen if you make a mistake, or what will happen if you are not perfect, guess what-you are going to make a mistake. If you change your thinking, you can change your life, but to do this you must be committed to your goal.

Every time a professional athlete enters a sports arena, he or she must possess the proper attitude, or that attitude could be their most fearless opponent. Athletes have a strong survival instinct, a killer's instinct, an-eat-or-be-eaten mentality. They wear their pride on their sleeves. Their athleticism is a defense from attackers. They protect their athletic crowns like a mother bear protecting her cubs. They have a winning mentality. If you want to win, you have to play like you mean it.

My attitude when I walk into the auditioning room to compete for an acting job is *I own this room and everything in it.* The job is mine to have. I must take it. You can adopt this attitude for any performing situation. I do not enter with an attitude that I am God's gift to acting. Do not mistake confidence for cockiness. I only use this as a way to solidify my confidence.

I once auditioned for a movie when I had laryngitis and could hardly speak, but I auditioned anyway. I got a callback. Then I got the job. My attitude and belief system is what gave me the courage to audition while sick.

I audition with no fear because I know that it is up to **me** to control the performing environment. You must seize the initiative and own the stage. When you show self-confidence the audience can feel it, in turn you can feel them. This simple give and take will help you be a better speaker.

Tips

- Visualize yourself captivating an audience.
- See them responding to you positively.
- Know that the audience came to see *you*. Give them what they need.
- Take time every day to tell yourself that you are equally competent as the best in your field. Then work, study, and practice to achieve it.
- Take time every day to feed your very powerful subconscious mind images of self-confidence and success because you are what you think. You will become what you wish.

Follow-up

Improvements I Can Make in This Area:

_____

_____

_____

_____

_____

_____

_____

Action Steps to Take:

_____

_____

_____

_____

_____

_____

_____

Results of Action Steps Taken:

_____

_____

_____

_____

_____

_____

_____

Chapter 3: Stage Fright:
What's The Worst Thing That Could Happen?

One of the biggest fears many of us have when it comes to public speaking is nervousness. Accompanying jittery nerves are things like fear of being embarrassed or humiliated, feeling out of control, becoming too petrified to speak, making a fool of ourselves by saying something silly, or making a mistake. Nerves are usually a result of thinking about the wrong thing...*yourself.* Saying things to yourself like, "I wonder how I will do? I hope I do not forget something; All of those people will be looking at me. What if I make a mistake? My boss is in the audience, what if I blow it?"

Take the focus off yourself and put it on the audience. Treat them as someone who needs your help, and help them.

Fear or stage fright is a thought and action annihilator. What is there to fear? It is perfectly normal and acceptable to get nervous before a performance. It is not acceptable to let your nerves control you. When you are unable to say what you are thinking or what you have planned to say, you allow a vital part of your individual personality to be arrested. The audience cannot and will not harm you. They want you to succeed. They do not want to feel uncomfortable because of your performance. View everyone in the audience as a friend. You know them better than you think you do.

An audience is a gathering of individuals with all the same elements of humanity:

- They have mothers and fathers
- They went to school with other kids
- They had problems with some kids
- They had a best friend
- They have had a piece of apple pie
- They got a bad grade
- They have had a cold drink on a hot day
- They have been yelled at by a parent
- They had a favorite toy
- They have been hugged

We are more alike than most of us think.

Nervousness induces shallow breathing. To combat it, breathe deeply, slowly, and expand your abdomen. Most of us wish we could lose a few pounds, and the last thing we want to do is go around sticking out our stomachs. Don't worry, the audience cannot see your midsection expanding before their eyes.

Fill your lungs with air, then fill your abdomen. (The abdomen does not really fill with air, but it will feel like it.) Picture your lungs with two upside-down hot-air balloons attached to the bottom of them. This provides added breathing capacity. Extending your abdomen and breathing from the bottom up is a form of **diaphragmatic breathing**, a technique used by the world's great singers and wind instrumentalists. Extending your abdomen has an overall quelling effect on the body. It also gives you a much larger pocket of air in the abdomen and the lungs from which to speak. This means you can speak longer without taking a breath. Breath control is important, ask any swimmer, runner, weight lifter or new mother.

Tips

- Being prepared is an antidote to nervousness.
- Know *why* you are addressing the group and keep that firmly in mind.
- Focus on the audience as an entity in need.
- Be anxious to satisfy their need.
- Do not focus on yourself. Thinking about yourself is why you are nervous.
- Focus on the needs of the audience.
- Focusing on yourself puts undue pressure on you. Remember *you* are not the reason you are there. The *audience* is.
- Know that the audience wants and needs your information.
- Speak to the audience as if you know them.
- Remember, the audience wants you to win. They are on your side!
- If the audience is giving you blank stares, do not translate that into, "They hate me, they think I am horrible, they want me out of here."
- Because the audience is not smiling and nodding at you does not mean that they do not "get it". Do not panic but stand your ground by remaining committed to your message.
- Extend your abdomen to allow extra breathing capacity to relax yourself.

Follow-up

Improvements I Can Make in This Area:

_____

_____

_____

_____

_____

_____

_____

_____

Action Steps to Take:

_____

_____

_____

_____

_____

_____

_____

Results of Action Steps Taken:

_____

_____

_____

_____

_____

_____

_____

Chapter 4: Pretend Sometimes:
Great Communicators Are Like Actors Playing a Role

Great actors have a thorough understanding of their material. They know and understand their audiences, the characters they are portraying, where the boundaries are, and where the buttons are and how to push them. Great actors are nearly fearless. They are not afraid to take risks and expose themselves.

There is a bit of the actor in all of us. Sometimes we have to "put it on" a little more than at other times. I am sure that this week you have said to someone you met for the first time, "Pleased to meet you." How do you know you are pleased to meet them? They could be one of the most vile people you have ever encountered, but you will not know that until you have spent more time talking with them. When we go to meetings, luncheons, and other events, a certain type of behavior is expected. We immediately adopt that behavior and "act" accordingly. We have learned that a little pretending can go a long way.

When you are presenting on stage, you do things you would not do in ordinary life. The audience does not care who you are in your other life. They just want you to give them something for their time spent with you right now. I often hear speakers say, "I can't do that, that is not me!" The audience does not care who you are or who you think you are. The audience wants to be rewarded for their time or money. So, give them a little something extra. You might even have to pretend to be having a good time.

Frank Sinatra said that you can't act like you're bored with the audience. Act like you love 'em. They'll love you back.

Tips

- Before addressing a group, elevate your mood. This will decrease the gap between pretending and your reality, which will make it easier to *pretend* if you have to.
- Develop your imagination: read science fiction and other imaginative works.
- Go to the art museum and think up stories, histories, and dialogue for the people in the paintings.
- View the works of artists such as Salvador Dali and Hieronymus Bosch. Then create improvised dialogue for their surrealistic characters and scenes.
- Study people in your everyday life, on the bus, in a store, or in a restaurant. Create a life, history, and a dialogue for them.
- You might have to pretend to be having a good time
- Be patient during interruptions
- Be enthusiastic for a product
- Be excited about your speech
- Be excited to be there

Follow-up

Improvements I Can Make in This Area:

_____

_____

_____

_____

_____

_____

_____

_____

Action Steps to Take:

_____

_____

_____

_____

_____

_____

_____

Results of Action Steps Taken:

_____

_____

_____

_____

_____

_____

_____

Chapter 5: The Meeting of The Minds:

Get Your Audience to Agree with You

To convince audiences to agree with us is the essence of the art of communication and persuasion. The sole focus and purpose of commercials is to get you to *agree* with the commercial, *believe* its content, and *buy* the product. The purpose of a film is to tell a story and have you *believe* the characters.

As a presenter, you constantly try to get others to agree with you, whether it is a speech to inform, educate, entertain, or inspire. You cannot get an audience to agree with you until you discover who they are and what they want. When you know what they want, the rest is easy. Either give it to them, or show them a way for them to get it for themselves. The best salespeople in any field know that they will be successful when they know and understand what their client wants. It is the same with persuasive speaking.

How do you get your audience's agreement? You achieve this by understanding the desires and fears of those who receive your message. When you understand what the receiver is already thinking, it is easy to supply more of what is already in their minds. When you show that you understand them and are more like them than they imagined, they will automatically let you in and grant you a passport to their hearts.

Tips

- Research your audience before the engagement.
- Know what your listener is thinking.
- Know what your listener wants.
- Know what your listener is afraid of.
- Discover ways to display to the audience that you are just like them.
- Speak to the audience and individuals as if you know them.

Follow-up

Improvements I Can Make in This Area:

_____

_____

_____

_____

_____

_____

_____

_____

Action Steps to Take:

_____

_____

_____

_____

_____

_____

_____

_____

Results of Action Steps Taken:

_____

_____

_____

_____

_____

_____

_____

_____

Chapter 6: Audience Research I:
Know Their Needs

Before you can provide the information your audience is seeking, you have to know who the audience is and what they want. If appropriate, interview the person hiring you before your engagement to learn the composition of the audience. Then customize information for them. Spend time meeting with audience members before your presentation. That will always give you key information to weave into your talk. Research the corporate culture, local culture, and community where you will be making your presentation.

President John F. Kennedy always knew how to construct his speeches and presentations because he would research the subject and audience thoroughly before making any statement to anyone. Lee Iacocca did extensive research on potential automobile purchasers in the mid-1960s before designing and producing the Mustang automobile. Because of his radio broadcasting and acting background, Ronald Reagan instinctively knew the importance of understanding the people on the other end of his communication.

One of the first lessons I teach my acting students is to know to whom you are speaking. That not only alters the content of the remarks, but the tone as well.

Tips

- Learn who your audience is before the speech. Relate to them. Know their age range, experience, goals for the day, expectations of you.
- Interview the person hiring you before your engagement and learn who the typical audience member is.
- Learn about the corporate culture where you will speak.
- Learn the name of key individuals and use some of them in your presentation.
- Learn details about key individuals and work it into your presentation.

Follow-up

Improvements I Can Make in This Area:

_____

_____

_____

_____

_____

_____

_____

Action Steps to Take:

_____

_____

_____

_____

_____

_____

_____

Results of Action Steps Taken:

_____

_____

_____

_____

_____

_____

_____

Chapter 7: Audience Research II:
Great Communicators Know to Whom They Are Speaking

Every actor in every film, play, soap opera, or commercial knows to whom they are speaking. A major part of communication and persuasion is being aware of who will be on the receiving end of the information you are giving. When researching a character they will portray, great actors uncover to whom they are speaking. Communication hinges on that discovery. You would speak differently to a policeman who is about to give you a speeding ticket for driving 70 mph in a 25 mph zone than you would to a five-year-old child who asks you how a butterfly comes from a caterpillar. Know to whom you are speaking, and speak to them accordingly. Knowing to whom you speak is a vital link to effective communication.

This lesson may be taken to the boardroom, meeting room, telephone, television, or the lectern. One exercise I give my acting students helps them break down their thoughts and perceptions into small, individual beats or segments. Create answers for each of these tips, and you will have additional tips for a better understanding of the audience, why you are there with them, and why they are there to hear you.

Tips

- Research your audience in advance.
- Know what your relationship is to the audience.
- Know what you have in common with the audience.
- Be clear in your mind as to how you communicate to the audience.
- Know what the audience is to you in your professional life.
- Know what the audience is to you in your personal life.
- Do you like the audience?
- Know why or why not.
- Know what you feel toward the audience.
- Know what you need from the audience.
- Know what you want the audience to think or feel about you.
- Know in what ways you are vulnerable to the audience.
- Know why you behave as you do toward the audience.
- Know what special aspects of yourself caused those feelings.
- Know what special aspects of yourself caused those needs.
- Be aware of the secrets on the subject that you know that the audience does not.
- Know what is left unsaid.
- Know how much of what you say is truthful.
- Know how much of what you say is cover-up.
- Role play with a colleague before your speaking engagement.

The more homework you do in advance, the better prepared and more confident you will be. You should be thinking about some of this information beforehand. This will help you be much better prepared to face any audience or individual for any purpose.

Follow-up

Improvements I Can Make in This Area:

_____

_____

_____

_____

_____

_____

_____

_____

Action Steps to Take:

_____

_____

_____

_____

_____

_____

_____

Results of Action Steps Taken:

_____

_____

_____

_____

_____

_____

_____

Chapter 8: Mental Pictures:
Feed Your Powerful Subconscious Mind

The business of presenting is a mental process. There is a technique that I have used for many years that I call *visualizing* or *projecting*. It is the process of using your imagination, inner vision, to see yourself successful at the end of your journey. This is a technique used often in the theater by stage actors. Film actors use it to picture their character in their minds well in advance of filming the project. Professional golfers, football players, gymnasts, basketball players, baseball players, tennis players, and many other professional athletes in recent years have started using this effective technique to their advantage. This is just one part of the power of positive thinking. You feed powerful, positive pictures or images to your subconscious mind, which gives the speaker confidence.

See yourself in front of a large audience hanging onto your every word. See yourself giving the audience great value for their time spent with you. See them loving you for it.

This technique will take some time to learn, but you will discover that it is well worth the effort. Please take the time to listen to a relaxation tape or CD when you have at least a half an hour or before bedtime. Allow yourself the time to fully implement this exercise.

Tips

- The more you think about achieving your goals, the more likely you are to achieve them.
- Listen to a relaxation CD when you have at least a half an hour or while lying in bed before going to sleep and think about what you want to achieve.
- Allow your mind to do the advance work for you. When it comes time for the actual execution, you will be much more confident.

Follow-up

Improvements I Can Make in This Area:

_____

_____

_____

_____

_____

_____

_____

_____

Action Steps to Take:

_____

_____

_____

_____

_____

_____

_____

_____

Results of Action Steps Taken:

_____

_____

_____

_____

_____

_____

_____

_____

Chapter 9: Now Breathe:
Relax the Body, Relax the Mind

Public speaking is stress inducing. The following exercises helps you relax your body and refresh your mind. They are often used in university acting programs. Some call them theater games, but there is nothing frivolous about them. They really work.

You can use this relaxation exercise before you introduce post relaxation suggestions and create images of success in your mind. If you follow these instructions closely, over time you will have positive results.

Exercise

- First, find a quiet place to perform this exercise. Lie on your back, hands at your side, or seat yourself in a comfortable chair with your hands placed palms down comfortably on your thighs and close your eyes.
- Concentrate on your breathing. Hear your breathing; think about it, each breath in, each breath out. Long, slow deep breaths. Think about your toes, and talk to them, tell them they are very relaxed, more relaxed than they have ever been.
- Use relaxing words like gentle, mild, soothing, smooth, droopy, lifeless, floppy, loose, slack, limp, fluffy, satiny, silky, velvety, cottony, mushy, flexible, liquid, malleable, pliable, delicate, elastic, feathery, rubbery, supple, pliant, flaccid, tender, soft, calm, serene, sedated, tranquil, peaceful, placid, mild, ease, oozing.

- Tell your toes they are melting on the bed sheet or on the floor; soft, warm, rubbery toes. Feel your toes respond to these suggestions. Enjoy the moment; know that your toes are truly more relaxed than they have ever been.
- Using the same imagery and words, work your way up the rest of your body, keeping the toes relaxed. Talk to your feet, and relax them. On to the ankles, then the calves and knees. Talk to your body slowly and confidently.
- Now, relax the front of your thighs, the back of your thighs, and buttocks. Think about what you are saying to your body. Know it. Believe it.
- Continue to listen to your breathing as you talk to and relax your abdomen, waist, and lower back. Move up into the chest area, shoulders, arms, biceps, triceps, forearms, and feel all of that negative, stressful energy leave your body through your finger tips.
- Because of the amount of stress this part of the body carries, we are going back to the upper back, shoulders, and neck. It is important that you relax these muscles because they are probably the most tense of the whole body.
- Relax the front of your neck, the back of your neck, the back of your head, the top of your head. Moving down to the forehead, the eyebrows, eyes, nose. Relax those tired cheeks from smiling all day. Relax your jaw muscles, lips, and chin.

Tips

- Study this exercise and repeat it frequently until it is memorized.
- Do this exercise daily for maximum results.
- Use this relaxation technique as preparation for any challenging task.

Think it, Become it

Now that you are relaxed, listen to your environment. Hear the birds, the traffic, the radio of your neighbor, the kids in the yard, the airplane passing overhead, the wind in the trees, your refrigerator humming. Be aware of your entire environment. After you have completely relaxed your entire body from your toes to your head, if you are not sleeping, this is where the fun begins.

Now is when you start to use mental imagery of success. Because you are now so relaxed, this is the time to put those powerful, positive images into your subconscious mind. Now is the time you should start to feed your mind the image of you the successful speaker or presenter. There is power in the details. Take the time to see the explicit detail of every scene.

Tips

In your mind:
- Picture the auditorium or meeting room.
- Count the steps up to the stage.
- Notice what kind of flooring is there.
- See what is on the wall in the background behind the lectern.
- See what kind of lectern is there.
- Picture the microphone.
- See the small light on the lectern to illuminate your script.
- Visualize the spotlight shining in your eyes.
- Notice the whole stage lit by overhead lights.
- See the audience.
- Hear the previous speaker introduce you.
- Hear the applause for you.

- Hear your introductory opening words.
- See yourself making valid points that the audience agrees with.
- Hear your closing remarks.
- See the audience burst into wild applause for your performance.

See the detail in your mind's eye. *See* these images and take note of your feelings. This is how you feed these powerful messages to your subconscious mind. Soon you will be able to do the imaging while walking down the street or driving your car, without the relaxation exercise. When the time comes for you to act on these images, it will be easy because you have done this work before, in your head. You have been there and you know what it feels like. You will be confident and on familiar territory.

Follow-up

Improvements I Can Make in This Area:

_____

_____

_____

_____

_____

_____

_____

_____

Action Steps to Take:

_____

_____

_____

_____

_____

_____

_____

_____

Results of Action Steps Taken:

_____

_____

_____

_____

_____

_____

_____

Section II
You...
The Presenter

Chapter 10:
Don't Just Stand There, Move:
Use Movement to Persuade

Movement creates excitement. Most scenes in film and television commercials are based on action. You capture interest when there is movement. In TV commercials, cereal boxes, soda cans, and bottles of dish washing liquid have movement. If the objects do not move, the director will zoom in or tilt the camera to give the illusion of movement. When this is done, it produces forward momentum and excitement.

The same thing should occur when you are behind the lectern. Speakers should create movement. When there is a lack of visual stimulation it is easy for an audience to mentally (or even physically) fall asleep. Movement works both in a large auditorium size room and a smaller office meeting room. Movement creates excitement and maintains audience interest.

Actors in film, theater, and television commercials are observers and students of human behavior. Their job is to re-create human characteristics. There is no better way to learn how humans move and behave than by observing them closely in their natural surroundings when they do not know they are being observed.

For the business professional who probably has not had acting training or experience, making a presentation can be a frightening experience. Many individuals address a group as if they were frightened beyond belief. That is because they probably are.

When we think of the "professional demeanor," we think of someone who is polished and poised. Many presidents and CEOs believe that if they are unemotional and aloof, they appear more leader-like and in control while displaying the "everything is fine" attitude. Actually, to really connect with an audience one-on-one, or with individuals in an office meeting environment, the less "stiff" you are the better. Your movement is key. Natural, believable movement is trustworthy. Non-jerky movement is secure and confident. If your body is believable the viewers will be open to you, listen to you, and trust you. Movement helps to maintain audience attention.

Tips

- Study the natural movement of people in everyday life.
- Use your upper torso with believable, natural, expressive movements.
- Use head movement, hand gestures, and facial expressions to help make your points.

Follow-up

Improvements I Can Make in This Area:

_____

_____

_____

_____

_____

_____

_____

_____

Action Steps to Take:

_____

_____

_____

_____

_____

_____

_____

_____

Results of Action Steps Taken:

_____

_____

_____

_____

_____

_____

_____

_____

Chapter 11: Own the Stage:
Ready? Action!

To many, the word **speech** means boredom. It means that someone is going to get up in front of the group and give a long, dull, lifeless talk that will put many in the audience to sleep. Actors, radio and TV hosts, successful political leaders, and other professional speakers often do not take ownership of the performing environment. They do not give themselves proper *permission* to perform the way they see the performance in their minds. Give yourself permission to be in the upper register of the dynamic range. In the upper ranges, you can scream and move about frantically if you wish. You must also give yourself permission to whisper or even stop speaking and moving all together. To do this is to operate in the lower register of the dynamic range. As the performer, you must be aware that this range is there for you to choose from.

There is an element of performance in effective public speaking. Do not deny yourself that opportunity. Do not think that you are not a performer. Do not say to yourself, "That is not me. I am not that way." You cannot *afford* to bore your audience. Actors often give their best performance in the elevator going down to the ground floor leaving a building or while driving home. That is because we are replaying the scene in our head, reliving the moment. We are performing in the elevator what should have been done in front of the camera or the audience.

Own the stage and take advantage. Know that you can do whatever you want, whenever you want. Just remember, *if you don't do it, it won't get done.*

Tips

- Develop empowering ways of thinking by seeing yourself as the speaker you want to become.
- Give yourself permission to perform the way you see the performance in your mind.
- Take charge of the environment by speaking in self-confident tones.
- Do not be afraid to raise your voice occasionally, but be sensitive as to when to lower it.

Follow-up

Improvements I Can Make in This Area:

_____

_____

_____

_____

_____

_____

_____

Action Steps to Take:

_____

_____

_____

_____

_____

_____

_____

Results of Action Steps Taken:

_____

_____

_____

_____

_____

_____

_____

Chapter 12: Eye Contact:
Engage Everyone

Have you ever noticed that actors almost always look at each other? That is the simplest and most direct way to make contact and engage the individuals you are addressing. The same element applies when addressing an audience: look at them, *all* of them. It is difficult to persuade someone if you are not looking right at them and engaging their attention. Many public speakers say to engage eye contact with the friendly faces in the audience. I say engage eye contact with the unfriendly faces. Those are **probably** the ones who need the most convincing. If you convince the most resistant, the rest is easy.

When presenting in a small room, it is important to take the time to look into the eyes of the individuals in your audience. When presenting to a larger audience, it is difficult for those in the audience to tell you are looking at them because there is someone directly in front of and behind them.

To make this work, break the audience into imaginary thirds. This will look like half of a pie chart cut into three equal triangles, or segments of the room. First, speak to the center of the room. Then turn your head slowly to the left and speak to that side of the room. Then slowly to the right and speak to that side. Do not stop at the center again before going to the right, point your head immediately to the right. Allow a few seconds to pass before making this left-to-right move. If you do not, it will look planned and contrived.

Normally our heads face forward. When the audience sees your head turn from far left to far right, they know you are looking at the entire room. This selection of audience segments will give your head more obvious movement and the appearance of talking to the entire room. This personalizes your talk and further engages the whole audience locking them into your content. If there is a spotlight on you, they will never know that all you see is a black wall of nothing.

Tips

- Make eye contact with your audience members to actively engage them.
- Before moving your head from left to right, maintain contact with that side of the room for several seconds, or until your thought has been completed.
- When blinded by a spotlight, do not scan the audience as if gazing into a faceless sea of humanity. Stop to engage individuals one on one, even when you cannot really see them.
- Treat the audience like a group of *individuals*, not an audience without names or faces.
- With a small group in a small room, the power of individual eye contact goes a long way. Make sure you use it.

Follow-up

Improvements I Can Make in This Area:

_____

_____

_____

_____

_____

_____

_____

_____

Action Steps to Take:

_____

_____

_____

_____

_____

_____

_____

Results of Action Steps Taken:

_____

_____

_____

_____

_____

_____

_____

Chapter 13: Lights! Camera! Now What?
TV Studios Frighten Me

You may have the occasion to speak or be interviewed on television. Television studios can be intimidating because our American culture has a strong focus on television and film. Many consider a television appearance to be a major accomplishment. It is easy to become caught up in the excitement of being on television and lose your focus, become nervous, and mishandle an important opportunity. The lights and television camera are partners in your performance—just like the microphone, they help you convey your message to your audience.

The main goal is always to look and sound real and natural. Knowing where and when to look into the television camera can make a tremendous difference in the audience's perception of you, your presentation, speech, or interview.

Tips

Before an interview or speech:

- Practice reading your script and looking up at the audience or into the camera giving eye or camera lens contact at key points.
- Prepare a few brief statements that make your key points and use them early in the interview.
- Prepare a brief list of benefits to the audience if they continue to listen to you, watch you, or buy your product.

- Create a brief list of benefits to buying or using your product and rotate them throughout the interview.
- Understand that the audience wants to like you. No matter what happens or what questions are asked, do not become abrasive or show anger.
- Know who the audience is and reward them for watching, listening, or reading the interview.
- Prepare yourself to compliment your competitor (if there is one) early in the interview.
- Prepare yourself to state your point in short "sound bite" sentences to avoid being misquoted.
- Know the topic of the interview in advance.
- Write a series of suggested questions for the interviewer and send them with a press kit a few days in advance of your appearance.
- Find out who is going to conduct the interview and if possible, study their style in advance.
- Do not assume that the reporter knows as much about your business as you do, they may not know anything. Be prepared to think on your feet and help them.
- Arrive at the TV or radio studio early to meet the host as soon as possible. Establishing a rapport off-camera or off-microphone will translate to *on*-camera or microphone.
- Be courteous to the media. They can make you or break you, but do not be a doormat.
- Do not allow the interviewer to have total control of the interview.
- Do not allow the interviewer to put words in your mouth.
- Do not be persuaded to change your opinion or position on a subject.
- Stop talking after you have made your point.
- Create at least three "worst-case scenario" or difficult questions you might be asked and have prepared answers for them.
- Videotape a mock interview with a friend to practice your relationship with the camera.

Tips

During an interview or speech:

- If there is competition there, compliment your competitor early in the interview.
- State your point in short "sound bite" sentences to avoid being misquoted.
- Do not keep talking after you have made your point. You could dig yourself into a hole.
- When there is a camera or a microphone present, there is no such thing as speaking "off the record." Always assume that recording equipment is ON.
- Have at least three messages or key points you want to convey, and seek an opportunity to state them early in the interview.
- If the interviewer asks a question and is then silent while maintaining direct eye contact with you, do not rush into an answer. This is a common tactic of journalists. Think before you speak.
- Do not use slang or too much inside industry jargon. Every member of the audience is not necessarily a member of your special club, and they will enjoy what you have to say a lot better if it is easy for them to understand.
- On a TV show where you are hosting the program or giving a speech, it is important to time your looks to the camera. Look up from your script during key points or at the end of certain sentences. Do not keep your head buried in the script and do not randomly look up at the audience.
- If you are being interviewed on a TV show, do not look into the camera. Look at the individual asking the questions, or look at other panel members when they are giving answers to questions.

- Understand that the audience wants to like you. No matter what happens or what questions are asked, do not become abrasive or show anger.
- Know who the audience is and be anxious to reward them for watching, listening, or reading the interview.
- Do not assume that the reporter knows as much about your business as you do. Be accommodating and help them along.
- Always be courteous to the media. They can make you or break you, but do not be a doormat.
- When answering questions, always look the interviewer in the eye.
- Do not allow the interviewer to have total control of the interview.
- Do not allow the interviewer to put words in your mouth.
- When being asked "theoretical" or "what if" questions, call it to their attention and be sure to state that it is a "theoretical" question. You do not have to answer.
- Do not answer any question that you do not want to. Say, "Next question please." Instead of, "No comment."
- Do not let an interviewer start an argument with you.
- Do not speak at the same time the interviewer is speaking. When two people speak at the same time, no one is heard.
- Use your list of benefits to the audience for continuing to listen to you, watch you, or buy your product. Rotate them throughout the interview.
- Always use your company or product name. Do not say "we" or "our product."

Follow-up

Improvements I Can Make in This Area:

_____

_____

_____

_____

_____

_____

Action Steps to Take:

_____

_____

_____

_____

_____

_____

Results of Action Steps Taken:

_____

_____

_____

_____

_____

_____

_____

Chapter 14: The Humanity Factor:
Don't Try to Be Perfect, Be Real

It is deeply ingrained in all of us that when we are in front of an audience, a camera, or a microphone, we should do something *special*, or be perfect. The opposite is true. Do **not** try to be perfect, for that will make you appear stiff. Why do we like or relate to some actors, speakers, or radio personalities better than others? Sometimes it is an unknown quality, or an intangible appeal that can be very elusive, but it is an important element in effective communication. It is important to learn how people in everyday life act, react, and respond. The more natural, calm, and at home you act the better you will be received. Move around if you can, use your hands, body, and facial expressions. The more still you are, the less interesting you will be to watch.

When you are speaking to your friends and relatives, you move your body, hands, and use facial expressions. When you are addressing a group, the same physical dynamic should be present. If you speak to the audience as you would your friends, the audience will be more likely to treat you like a friend.

Tips

- An element of performance should be present when addressing a group.
- Use your natural habits while addressing a group. Walk, talk, and make use of your body, as you would while talking to one friend.
- Laugh at yourself if you make a mistake. It will make you look more real.
- Tell a personal anecdote. Show that you are just like the audience.
- Speak to the audience as if you know them.

Follow-up

Improvements I Can Make in This Area:

_____

_____

_____

_____

_____

_____

_____

_____

Action Steps to Take:

_____

_____

_____

_____

_____

_____

_____

_____

Results of Action Steps Taken:

_____

_____

_____

_____

_____

_____

_____

Chapter 15:
Dialogue, Monologue, Vocal Image:
Judged by What You Say and How You Say It

Great actors and great communicators use their voices and inflections as tools of communication and persuasion. They use good diction and volume. There is no communication if the potential receiver of your message cannot understand what you are saying. Great communicators shape, color, and punch their words for maximum impact. Speech is verbal music. You will learn to make your words sing.

Many elements determine the sound of your speech. The main elements are volume, silence or pauses, rate of speech, pitch, inflection, pronunciation, and breath control.

Volume: It is important to learn vocal volume control. You can convey a tremendous amount of meaning simply by increasing or decreasing volume. Take any piece of copy, page from your speech or newspaper and read a line from it aloud. Say the line in soft, hushed, quiet tones first. Then say the same line with half again as much volume. Notice the change in tone. Say it again with twice as much volume and note the change. You are saying the same words, but your use of volume gives it an entirely different meaning.

The wonderful English actor John Houseman as professor Kingsfield in the movie *The Paper Chase* said, "Fill the room with your intelligence."

Tips

- Use your dynamic range. Explore your volume possibilities.
- Speak loudly to be heard, softer to be expressive.
- If your voice has a problem reaching the back of the room, visually focus on the back of the room and speak to a person sitting there.
- Use a tape recorder to listen to and study your work.

Silence or pauses: There is power in the pause. Pauses create suspense and interest, and you should learn how to use them in your presentations. It is an easy method of getting the listener's attention. Just as in music, the notes that are *not* played, or the spaces of emptiness or silence, has just as much significance as the notes that *are* played. When radio and TV broadcasters speak, there are few pauses or hesitations. But actors often use silence and pauses to punctuate their sentences.

Tips

- Take a line from this page, your prepared speech, or a printed page from a magazine or newspaper and read it aloud.
- First, read the line all together, linking one word to the next without significant pauses.
- Now say the same line broken up with pauses of silence at strategic places. You will hear how the use of pauses and silence can be used to get the attention of the listener.
- Use a tape recorder to hear and study your work.

Grouping: This is a method used to create an ebb and flow of words. It attracts attention and prevents boredom, even if you have a monotone voice. To group words, you take a series of words and say them rapidly in a group together. This will allow the words that are not grouped to stand out and be heard more clearly.

Read this sample sentence all together without stopping:

It is often much easier to get a reaction from a large audience than a smaller one because they all feed off one another, and the sound they make together is amplified by their sheer numbers.

Read this sample sentence while grouping the parts together located within the brackets: [*It is often much easier to get a reaction*]*...from...a...larger...audience...///...than...a...smaller...one* [*because they all feed off one another, and the sound they make together*] *is... amplified...by their...sheer...numbers.*

Tips

- The words that are not grouped together must be spoken slowly and deliberately for maximum impact.
- Use a tape recorder to hear and study your work.
- Grouping is a powerful tool, learn to master it.

Rate of speech: Slow speech can bore the listener. Rapid speech makes you sound nervous and out of control. To maintain an interesting sound, vary your rate. Studies have shown ordinary conversation to be between 150 and 200 words per minute. Very few people know their rate of speech, but we all recognize when someone is talking too fast or too slowly. We can mentally process information faster than we can speak.

Tips

- Pace the delivery of your words.
- Use a tape recorder to discover a comfortable rate for you.

- Learn to add or subtract space between your words to speedup or slow-down your delivery.

Pitch of the voice: How high or low you speak is the *pitch* of your voice. Subtleties between high and low create shading, coloring, and shaping. Pitch is another effective tool used to make specific impact on the audience without them knowing it. If you are nervous, the pitch can rise. If you force it too low, you can sound affected and unnatural. The pitch used can also alter the implied meaning of a word.

Tips

- Gather some reading material. Select one or two sentences and vary the pitch on specific words. Try to alter the meaning by changing your pitch.
- Draw arrows next to the words to be emphasized.
- Perform your reading into a tape recorder.
- Study how real people speak versus how newscasters speak.

Inflection: The change in pitch is the inflection. Inflection allows you to differentiate between a question and a statement. Example:
You're going to the office? ↗ You're going to the office. ↘
Inflections can also make you sound happy or sad, sincere or sarcastic. The last thing you want to do is use the wrong inflection at the wrong time. Beginning voice actors often have a problem adding inflection to their work. Speaking without inflection or changing pitch is delivering a flat, monotone read. Having a command of inflection variations can pay off handsomely.

Tips

- Gather reading material. Select one or two sentences and vary the inflection on specific words. Try to alter the meaning by changing your inflection.
- Draw arrows next to the words to be emphasized.
- Perform your reading into a tape recorder.

Pronunciation: Mispronunciation is saying a word incorrectly. Like saying gen-u-*wine* instead of genuine (*gen*-u-win.) Another example is saying "duh" instead of "the," "nim" or "dem" instead of "them," "dis" instead of "this."

If you have a regional accent, like a Boston, Texas, or New York accent, I recommend learning standard American speech pronunciation. I am not suggesting that you lose your accent. Just add an additional way of speaking. If you have a foreign accent, the same thing applies.

Tips

- Always have a dictionary nearby to verify proper pronunciation.
- Learn a new word every week, then increase your learning to every day.
- Study national network television broadcasters' style of speaking and their pronunciation.

Articulation: A lazy mouth or lazy tongue is often the cause of in-articulation. The failure to properly use the lips, teeth, tongue, jaw, and muscles of the cheeks to form one's words can cause misunderstanding. It is common to mumble or slur one's words, but this is not acceptable as a professional speaker. It is important to know how to say "didn't" instead of "dint," "ought to" instead of "otta," "have to" instead of "hafta," "going to" instead of "gonna," "want to" instead of "wanna," and so on.

Tips

- Place a wine bottle cork in your mouth, then read something aloud. Try to properly pronounce each word. This retrains your lips, tongue, and cheeks for proper speech.
- Do the EEE-OOO exercise. Put your mouth in an extreme and exaggerated smile while saying a series of the letter "E" all together for several seconds. Then radically purse and thrust your lips forward saying a series of the letter "O." Then alternate E-O-E-O-E-O. This will loosen the facial muscles to aid in crisper articulation.

Breath control: Imagine your lungs as two upside down hot air balloons extending down into your abdomen. First, fill your lungs with air, and then extend your abdomen filling your stomach with air (the abdomen does not really fill with air, but it will feel like it). Actually, you are expanding your diaphragm. This is a technique used by singers and wind instrumentalists known as diaphragmatic breathing. This will allow you to speak longer without taking a breath, giving you more control. It also helps you relax and prevents shallow breathing, which is a major contributor to stage fright.

Tips

- Practice this breathing technique while seated at your desk. The more you practice it, the more refined your technique will be when you need it.
- Get a stop watch or a clock with a second hand. Fill your lungs with air and time your slow exhalation until your lungs are empty. Do the same thing again, but extend your abdomen and fill your lungs and extend your abdomen this time. Notice the time difference.
- Do the same exercise while reading a passage aloud.

Follow-up

Improvements I Can Make in This Area:

_____

_____

_____

_____

_____

_____

_____

_____

Action Steps to Take:

_____

_____

_____

_____

_____

_____

_____

_____

Results of Action Steps Taken:

_____

_____

_____

_____

_____

_____

_____

Chapter 16: Your Script, Your Business:
No One Knows What You Are Going To Say

No one knows what you are going to say or what you have planned. If you miss a word, phrase, or paragraph, no one will know. Just keep going. The exception is if you miss an important fact, you should correct it. You are in control. Armed with the knowledge that you are in control can make you fearless.

Because it *is* your script, be sure you can read it. Double space your script and use a larger font if you use a word processor. If not, take it to a copy center and have your script enlarged. Use a serif typeface like this: abcdefg. Do not use a sans serif typeface like this: abcdefg, or **ALL CAPS: ABCDEFG**. When your eyes scan across the words, you see that some letters are raised above others. If they are all the same height you have to concentrate harder to distinguish each letter. This makes you slow down to recognize each word. Sans serif typeface does not have the little extensions, or legs on the letters. The use of a sans serif typeface in all capital letters is not what we usually see when reading the newspaper, magazines, books, brochures, or newsletters. That minor detail could be just enough to break your concentration and completely throw you off your performance.

Very little of the materials we read everyday is in sans serif type or all capital letters. This could throw us a bit when referring to our script or notes while delivering a speech. The most common typeface is *probably* Times New Roman or something similar. Use it.

Tips

- If working with your script at the lectern, make sure the typeface is large enough to read in a dimly lit room.
- Use a highlighter to indicate key points in your script.
- If you miss a point or miss a word, *just keep going.* It sounds worse if you go back and correct the mistake. It draws attention to it. Very good broadcasters never stop to correct their mistakes.
- If you get a **fact** wrong, you must stop to correct that.
- You have the script, you have the agenda, you control what you say, when you say it, and how long you say it.

Follow-up

Improvements I Can Make in This Area:

_____
_____
_____
_____
_____
_____
_____
_____

Action Steps to Take:

_____
_____
_____
_____
_____
_____
_____
_____

Results of Action Steps Taken:

_____
_____
_____
_____
_____
_____
_____
_____

Chapter 17: Communi-tainment:

Entertain While Communicating

All forms of media use humor. The movies, television shows, and commercials. Humor is an accessible, acceptable form of communication acknowledged by all. Humor is an attempt to reach out, communicate, and persuade. The audience knows that, and they will feel your goodwill and support you. It is a sure way of winning audience approval and attention. You will appear relaxed, in control of yourself, and ultimately in control of the audience.

Be cautious. You should monitor your humor and strategically place it according to your needs and propriety. Humor as a prosecuting attorney in the courtroom? I think not. You do not want to appear to not take the situation seriously. Humor in a business meeting can be used to prevent boredom, display humanity, and maintain interest. This can be an inconspicuous tool used to make your points with the audience.

It is a common practice to open a speech or presentation with a humorous anecdote. However, this could backfire on you. You could create unfulfilled expectations in the audience. It is easy to open with a bang and close with a whimper. Make sure you have follow-up material. If you do not feel comfortable with humor, *do not use it*. It is too easy to fall on your face.

Tips

- Use humor to make your audience feel comfortable with you, when they are comfortable with you, their guard is down making it easier to communicate with them.
- Use humor as an icebreaker to cut tension or relieve nervousness.
- The best use of humor is as it relates to the subject on which you are currently speaking. Otherwise, it sounds like a joke for the sake of a joke.
- If you are not a funny person, and you choose to use humor, space it out and use it throughout your presentation instead of using only a humorous opening.
- If you are not comfortable with humor, do not use it. If you are not a good joke teller, don't even try.

Follow-up

Improvements I Can Make in This Area:

_____

_____

_____

_____

_____

_____

_____

_____

Action Steps to Take:

_____

_____

_____

_____

_____

_____

_____

Results of Action Steps Taken:

_____

_____

_____

_____

_____

_____

_____

Chapter 18: The Emotion Potion:

Use the Emotional Connection

To be a great communicator you must bring an emotional connection into your speech or talk. Dale Carnegie said, "When dealing with people, remember you are not dealing with creatures of logic, but with creatures of emotion."

When creating your talk, you can use universal themes, like food, family, fun, and love. The film *Love Story* with Ali McGraw and Ryan O'Neil had an obvious tear-jerking twist built on a universal theme—love and love lost. *Titanic* with Leonardo DiCaprio and Kate Winset—love and love lost. While researching the response to Steven Spielberg's film *Shindler's List*, the emotions ran the gamut, depending on the individual's connection to the Holocaust. Striking an emotional chord is a key element to guaranteed communication.

Any of the Hallmark card TV commercials, most Mother's Day, Valentine's Day, wedding commercials, and commercials with babies, all have a high level of persuading emotional content. Major companies have spent hundreds of millions of dollars on product and audience research looking for key elements to contribute to increased sales. When researchers discovered the element of the audience's *emotional response* to a product or scene in a commercial, they discovered the key element to the consumer's psyche and ultimately, their wallets.

Many of the great speeches and speakers of our time have a high level of emotional content. Some examples of individuals to read are:

- Golda Meir, who said, "Those who do not know how to weep with their whole heart don't know how to laugh either."
- Ex-New York Governor Mario Cuomo speaks of his upbringing as an immigrant from a poor family whose first language was Italian, and making it in spite of that limitation.
- The Dr. Martin Luther King Jr.'s "I Have a Dream" speech, in which he said, "Injustice anywhere is a threat to justice everywhere."
- Mother Teresa, who said, "I am a little pencil in the hand of a writing God who is sending a love letter to the world."

Tips

Appeal to any one or all of these basic needs of most people:
- The desire to be loved and emotionally nurtured.
- The instinct for survival and safety.
- The need to feed the ego.
- The need for pleasure.

Follow-up

Improvements I Can Make in This Area:

_____

_____

_____

_____

_____

_____

_____

_____

Action Steps to Take:

_____

_____

_____

_____

_____

_____

_____

_____

Results of Action Steps Taken:

_____

_____

_____

_____

_____

_____

_____

Chapter 19: Once Upon a Time...
Tell a Story with a Beginning, a Middle, and End

"Once upon a time" is a phrase that will live forever. There is little more persuasive than a good story. Every story must have a beginning, a middle, and end. Boy meets girl. Boy marries girl. Boy and girl live happily ever after. Beginning, middle, and end. Every business presentation or speech must have the same components.

Personal stories are easy to relate to. Do not use stories for the sake of stories. Make sure they are appropriate and connected to your topic. They engage your audience and many audience members will see themselves in your stories.

Tips

- Stories are very useful in helping you persuade your audience. Learn to weave them into your presentations.
- Use the familiar order of stories to prevent audience confusion and to help maintain their attention.
- Use stories to comfort and reinforce audience's existing beliefs.
- Use stories to help audiences use their imagination and *see* what you are talking about.
- Make your stories visual. Audiences remember speeches that have a visual component to them.
- Use stories to impart information more clearly.

- Be aware of the stories that unfold before you in your everyday life.
- Use personal stories to help the audience relate to you and understand your message.

Business people, marketers, or sales managers can learn a lot about storytelling by watching the film work of some of our greatest artists of the craft.

- Frank Capra—*Mr. Smith Goes to Washington, It's a Wonderful Life.*
- Steven Spielberg—*Hook*, The *Indiana Jones* series, *Shindler's List.*
- George Lucas—The *Star Wars* series.

Review the works of other creative artists, such as songwriters and novelists. This will help you bring the important art of storytelling to your meetings and presentations.

Follow-up

Improvements I Can Make in This Area:

_____

_____

_____

_____

_____

_____

_____

_____

Action Steps to Take:

_____

_____

_____

_____

_____

_____

_____

_____

Results of Action Steps Taken:

_____

_____

_____

_____

_____

_____

_____

_____

Chapter 20: Nonverbal Dialogue:
Your Body Speaks Volumes

The body has a mind of its own. It can telegraph messages we do not intend. If the speaker is saying one thing and his or her body says another, the audience tends to focus on what the body is saying rather than the words spoken. Speakers who know how to gesture and use body language effectively are persuasive speakers.

It is important to gesture when speaking, but do not use gestures for the sake of gestures. Your words will dictate what your body does. If the gesture is real, natural, and believable, use it. If you are *planning* gestures, *don't*, they will appear phony. Allow them to happen on their own. You do not want your gestures to call attention to themselves, but to reinforce your ideas. This is an ideal opportunity to display your humanity; do not overrehearse in this area. Use your hands in natural, calming ways. Do not point at the audience, or raise the index finger unless referring to the number one.

Pointing is accusatory, negative, too strong, and pushy. Instead, if you must point, open the hand with the palm facing up and use the index finger in a curled and loose position. I prefer to point my palm to the left, right, or straight up. Once you have done this, do not just leave the hand there. Move it around, or it looks affected. Using these gestures opens you up and makes you appear more giving, vulnerable, and appealing.

Tips

- Always spend time studying the movements of real people in everyday situations.
- When you speak to friends and relatives, you use your body and facial expressions. The same should be done when addressing a group or a camera.
- Videotape yourself making an improvised speech moving as naturally and fluidly as you can without planning gestures.
- Do not plant your feet shoulder width apart evenly on the floor. This will make you look less comfortable. Stand with your weight on one leg and shift occasionally. The key is, the less stiff and rigid you are the more believable you will be.

Follow-up

Improvements I Can Make in This Area:

_____
_____
_____
_____
_____
_____
_____
_____

Action Steps to Take:

_____
_____
_____
_____
_____
_____
_____
_____

Results of Action Steps Taken:

_____
_____
_____
_____
_____
_____
_____
_____

Chapter 21: Put Your Best Look Forward:
You Are Judged Before You Speak

If you wear the wrong clothes to your presentation, the clothes will enter the room five minutes before you do. Even when you are not performing, someone is watching you. Your wardrobe is an important communication and persuasion tool.

I have a friend who is a professional wardrobe stylist for film, commercials, and major television projects. She once told me that it is important to know your coloring and the colors that look good on you. That is an easy way to look good without anyone else knowing why.

WOMEN

Fortunately for women, there are far more fashion and style options available than for men. Unfortunately, that means that mistakes are easier to make.

Tips on Color

- For your live presentations or television appearances, white is too bright and reflects too much light back to the audience or camera lens.
- Red is a great color for a live presentation because it is easy to spot you unless you are against a red background. Red is not good for television. It can make you look larger than you really are.

- Most shades of gray and shades of blue work well for TV.
- If you have gray or blonde hair, do not wear pastel shades. Wear something with color that will enliven your look.

Tips on Patterns

- For television, never wear small checks, herringbone, small polka dots, small stripes, or small plaid. The pattern can "move" even when you are not.
- Solid colors with texture but with no pattern work best on TV.
- If there are other people on the program, the director could have the camera focus on someone else because of the offensive pattern on your clothes. You will lose valuable on-camera time.

Tips on Hair

- Your hairstyle should be business not a party style and should flatter your face.
- Do not allow your hairstyle to hide your face. It is important for your face to be seen, especially on television.
- For television, it is important to keep your hair away from your face. Otherwise, it can create shadows on your face and hide your eyes.

Tips on Make-up

- Make-up for live presentations or television should not be heavy nightclub style, but business style. Less is more.

- If you apply your own make-up, use only enough to flatter, and only enough powder to prevent a shiny face. The shine makes you look nervous.
- When applying your make-up, make sure your neck color matches your face color.
- When applying your make-up do not use too much lighter make-up under the eye to de-emphasize bags. With TV lighting, it can give you a raccoon look.
- When making TV appearances, use their professional make-up artist.
- If you are an author, make sure you get a manicure before appearing on television. They could get a close-up of you holding the book and your nails will appear in an extreme close-up shot.

Tips on Jewelry

- Some common jewelry mistakes are large, flashy gold chains and necklaces. They can be visually distracting to viewers.
- Long, dangling earrings can be distracting.
- Avoid loose and noisy bangle bracelets. They could make unwanted noises.
- Large jewelry can create bad reflections from television lights.

Tips on Glasses

- Use reflection-free lenses for your glasses for television use.
- If you have a vision problem but do not want to wear glasses while on-camera, investigate contact lenses.
- You may wear only one contact lens. The brain decides which eye it will use, the one with the contact lens or the one without.
- Make sure your frame style flatters your face and is not outdated.

Tips on Shoes

- The *style* of your shoes should compliment your outfit.
- The *color* of your shoes should compliment your outfit.
- For important engagements do not wear shoes that have never been worn before. Comfort is an important issue. You do not want to be nervous *and* uncomfortable with aching feet.

MEN

Tips on Color and Patterns

- For television, never wear small checks, herringbone, small polka dots, small stripes, or small plaid. The pattern can "move" even when you are not.
- Solid colors with texture but with no pattern work best on TV.
- If there are other people on the program, the director could have the camera focus on someone else because of the offensive pattern on your clothes. You will lose valuable on-camera time.
- Men should wear medium or dark suits. Never light or pastel.
- If you have gray or blond hair, do not wear pastel shades. Wear something with color that will enliven your look.
- Your socks should be navy blue or black to match your suit and should be long enough to cover your leg when seated when your pants ride up.

Tips on Ties

- Conservative ties work best for live presentations or television interviews. Do not wear your party tie.
- Your tie should touch your belt, not too much below, definitely not above.
- A brightly colored tie, but not with wild patterns, with a dark suit is striking and effective.
- Small check patterns can "move" even when you are not moving.
- Your throat can make a bow tie move when you speak; wear them with caution.

Tips on Shirts

- White shirts are the staple for business, but they do not work well on television. They are too bright for the lights.
- Wear a light blue shirt instead of white when going on-camera.
- If you must wear a pocket-square or handkerchief, choose a color other than white.
- Do not forget collar stays. Curling collars are very ugly in person and on television.

Tips on Jewelry

- If you wear jewelry, keep it to small jewelry only. The less you wear, the better.
- Tie clasps, medallions, and chains should be avoided. They can make distracting sounds or create reflections.

Tips on Glasses

- Use reflection-free lenses for your glasses for television use.
- If you have a vision problem but do not want to wear glasses while on-camera, investigate contact lenses, or using one contact lens for reading and the naked eye for distance.
- Make sure the frame style of your glasses flatters your face and is not outdated.

Tips on Shoes

- The *style* of your shoes should compliment your outfit.
- The *color* of your shoes should compliment your outfit.
- Your shoes should be shined. Scruffy looking shoes are a telling sign of **something**.
- For important engagements do not wear shoes that have never been worn before. Comfort is an important issue. You do not want to be nervous *and* uncomfortable with foot pain.
- Shoes and belt color should match.

Tips on Makeup

- When making TV appearances, use the station's professional makeup artist.
- If you are an author, make sure you get a manicure before appearing on television. They could get a close-up of you holding the book and your nails will appear in an extreme close-up shot.

- If you apply your own makeup, use only enough to flatter, and only enough powder to prevent a shiny face. The shine makes you look nervous.
- When applying your makeup, make sure your neck color matches your face color.
- When applying your makeup do not use too much lighter makeup under the eye to de-emphasize bags. With TV lighting, it can give you a raccoon look.

Follow-up

Improvements I Can Make in This Area:

_____
_____
_____
_____
_____
_____
_____

Action Steps to Take:

_____
_____
_____
_____
_____
_____
_____

Results of Action Steps Taken:

_____
_____
_____
_____
_____
_____
_____

Chapter 22: Don't Forget!
Memorization Techniques

Have you ever been awed as actors recite extensive dialogue before your eyes? How do they do that, how do they memorize all those words?

Your memory is like a muscle. The more you exercise it, the stronger it gets. If you want to work from memory instead of note cards or a script, much preparation is needed.

One of the main jobs of actors is to memorize their scripts. There are many ways to do this. If you have to memorize, here are some tips to help you achieve that.

Tips

- Walking while memorizing helps you retain the information. You can do this either while walking on a busy city street, down a quiet country lane, or pacing in one small room.
- Memorizing while in the gym on the Stairmaster, treadmill, exercise bike, or rowing machine are all very effective because of the walking motion.
- Record your dialogue with a tape recorder. Then play it back and recite aloud along with it. This gives you a chance to both *see* and *hear* the words.
- Affix images to specific words or groups of words. Using mental pictures will help trigger the necessary words of your dialogue.

- Work on dialogue while lying in bed just before you go to sleep, then again the first thing in the morning.
- The old-fashioned way of simply constantly repeating the dialogue numerous times until you feel comfortable with it always works.
- Memorize by association, replacing the real word with a word or phrase to help you remember the original word or phrase.

Follow-up

Improvements I Can Make in This Area:

_____

_____

_____

_____

_____

_____

_____

Action Steps to Take:

_____

_____

_____

_____

_____

_____

_____

Results of Action Steps Taken:

_____

_____

_____

_____

_____

_____

Chapter 23: Lifetime Rehearsals:
How Do You Get to Carnegie Hall?

To become proficient at anything takes practice and rehearsals. Becoming a great speaker does not happen overnight, so nix the quick fix. Few are willing to put in the hard work that is really necessary to achieve greatness. You cannot take one or two coaching sessions and expect to become an instant expert. If you expect to stand out from the crowd, you must work harder than the crowd.

Practicing a speech is important. Certainly, this can be embarrassing in front of family members. Speaking aloud in an empty room is not something we normally do. I myself do it all the time. I read signs aloud while walking down the street. I read newspapers, magazines, and books aloud. I am *always* practicing and rehearsing. I repeat lines of dialogue from radio and television aloud. You have to hear yourself speaking the lines; do not do this exercise silently. You cannot be shy.

Tips

- Use mental imagery to see an audience before you and speak to them.
- When possible read in front of real people, family members, or neighbors.
- Tape-record and critically listen to your work.
- When possible, always read aloud. You need to become accustomed to the sound of your voice and projecting to the back of a room.
- Be aware that the written word sounds different when you are *speaking* them than when you are reading them to yourself.

Follow-up

Improvements I Can Make in This Area:

_____

_____

_____

_____

_____

_____

_____

Action Steps to Take:

_____

_____

_____

_____

_____

_____

_____

Results of Action Steps Taken:

_____

_____

_____

_____

_____

_____

_____

Section III
Your Hardware

Chapter 24: The Power of Color:
Use Color to Persuade and Sell

Two key elements in television and film production are color and movement. Color can be a persuasive and seductive tool. Primary (red, yellow, and blue) colors are the most important. They are eye catching and stimulating. All other colors are made from the primary ones. When used in their brighter shades these colors subconsciously take us back to our childhood. Making subtle childhood connections with an audience can really work to your advantage.

Take time to study television commercials; you will notice massive amounts of color in most of them. Color in the product, the background, the actor's wardrobe, and the graphics. When you create your business presentations, make sure that color is part of your presentational mix. The era of the black-and-white overhead is gone. The colors of the clothes you wear, the color scheme of the room you are in, the colors in your visual aids…you must consider all of these. Color can have a powerful and persuasive impact on the viewer. Use it.

Tips

- Use color for your overheads and all visual presentations.
- Use color in your wardrobe.
- Study TV commercials to see what colors are being used today.
- Research the color scheme of the room to coordinate with your wardrobe.

Follow-up

Improvements I Can Make in This Area:

_____

_____

_____

_____

_____

_____

_____

Action Steps to Take:

_____

_____

_____

_____

_____

_____

_____

Results of Action Steps Taken:

_____

_____

_____

_____

_____

_____

_____

Chapter 25: The Lectern:
Petrified Wood

The lectern was designed to hold your script, speech, or book from which you are reading. It was not designed to hold your hands, arms, or elbows. However, notice that President Clinton holds on to the sides of the lectern all the time. If you have the option to work without it, do so. You can become more mobile, creating much-needed movement and energy.

The lectern can make you appear stiff and stilted. It blocks part of the necessary communication between you and your audience. Work to control it, not be controlled by it. The lectern acts as the bottom quarter of a framing device, as in a picture frame, or a television set. The imagination of the viewer supplies the rest of the frame. It is your duty to "agitate" this frame, cause it to move. Do not allow yourself to be a stiff and lifeless object in the middle of the frame, lulling the audience to sleep.

Tips

- The more upper body movement you have while behind the lectern, the less static your visual presence. Remember the lectern does not move and movement creates excitement.
- Do not hold onto the sides of the lectern. It makes you look nervous and uncertain.
- Pound on the lectern only for **very strong** emphasis. This could be off-putting to some audience members.
- While behind the lectern, use the four fingers of one hand in a spread piano playing position to mark the location on your script if you are reading it. It will help you find your place faster.

Follow-up

Improvements I Can Make in This Area:

_____

_____

_____

_____

_____

_____

_____

Action Steps to Take:

_____

_____

_____

_____

_____

_____

_____

Results of Action Steps Taken:

_____

_____

_____

_____

_____

_____

_____

Chapter 26: Microphones:
Types and Tips

Microphones intimidate many people. You should view the microphone as a friend who is helping your audience hear your message.

It helps amplify and deliver your message to your waiting audience. Spend time performing a sound check before your presentation. When levels are properly adjusted, your voice will be heard clearly throughout the entire room. If the microphone is attached to the lectern, do not try to lean into it to get closer, hoping to be heard better. That will spoil your posture, make you look awkward, and will not make your voice any louder or clearer.

There are various types of microphones with varying frequency responses and sensitivities. Some are directional, some are nondirectional. A directional microphone has to be pointed directly and fairly close to your mouth. A nondirectional microphone can pick up your voice from a greater distance and does not have to be as close to your mouth.

Tips

- **Stand-up** microphones will force you to stand in one place, but you can often remove it to a hand-held position. This microphone should be spoken into from an angle, especially if it does not have a foam rubber windscreen on it. It is easy to get those annoying "plosive or popping" sounds without one. Speaking too closely into this type of microphone will also create those unwanted sounds.

If you have the occasion to move your head from one side to the other to look at the audience on either side, make sure that your mouth does not move away from the microphone. Your mouth must remain pointed in the direction of the microphone or the volume will diminish.

- **Hand-held** microphones give speakers the most freedom to move about. It can be difficult to control the distance to your mouth, therefore the volume can vary. Sometimes this style of microphone can hit against jewelry or clothing and make unwanted noises. You should never speak too closely or directly into the front of it.

- **Clip-on** microphones are most common on TV. If you plan to wear a broach or a pin, be aware that the microphone may provide visual competition or confusing clutter on your chest. If you will be walking around, please secure the cord with tape on the back of your garment. It is easy to trip on the cord or get it tangled.

- **Lavaliere** microphone is a type of clip-on microphone. They are usually mounted on a wire that is secured around your neck. The same cord problem can exist as with the clip-on microphone. They are usually of good quality and you can speak in a normal tone.

- **Stationary** microphones are affixed to the lectern or a desk. You usually are not able to adjust them, and they restrict your movement. The most common problem with this type of microphone is people leaning in to speak. Do not fall into this trap. Though it appears far away from you, it can pick you up clearly. Do not shout, and do not lean forward.

Follow-up

Improvements I Can Make in This Area:

_____

_____

_____

_____

_____

_____

_____

_____

Action Steps to Take:

_____

_____

_____

_____

_____

_____

_____

_____

Results of Action Steps Taken:

_____

_____

_____

_____

_____

_____

_____

Chapter 27: Room Acoustics:
Know How Sound Travels in the Room

Knowing the performance room's acoustic dynamics and other features of the environment make you seem aware and professional. Ridding the environment of any traps, such as an inadequate sound system, loud fan, or being near a loud and, busy kitchen, will help make your presentation go smoothly. Do not mention any inconveniences for which you do not have preplanned remedies.

Take time to review the physical properties of the room. If the room has wall-to-wall carpeting with no windows and a low ceiling, it is probably a low-bass-sounding or *dead* room. Sound will not travel very easily. Carpeting, curtains, and upholstered chairs all soak up sound, which creates a dead or soft room. To be heard more clearly, you will probably have to speak a little louder. On the other hand, a room that has bare windows, high ceilings, hardwood, tile, or marble floors, is very alive and reflective, or a **hard** room. Sound echoes and travels readily in an environment like this. The louder you speak, the more distorted and difficult to understand you may become.

Tips

- Arrive early before your presentation to analyze the room and actually speak with and without the microphone turned on.
- The acoustics of the room will change when it is filled with people, be prepared to readjust your speaking volume accordingly.
- Take the time to double-and triple-check the sound system and projectors for your visual aids to make sure they are all working properly.
- Contact the banquet or facility manager to correct any problems.

Follow-up

Improvements I Can Make in This Area:

_____

_____

_____

_____

_____

_____

_____

Action Steps to Take:

_____

_____

_____

_____

_____

_____

_____

Results of Action Steps Taken:

_____

_____

_____

_____

_____

_____

_____

Chapter 28: Telephone as a Tool:
Your Power in Voice-Only Communication

More important than the microphone is the telephone. It is a more common part of your personal and professional life. Fax and email are viable means of communication today, but the telephone is still the most often used. In written communication you will write and rewrite sentences several times before they are final. In speech communication, you do not have that luxury. Career advancement today is not possible without good telephone skills.

As a business professional, your vocal image is very exposed because of frequent telephone contact. It is important that you are aware of what you say, how you say it, and how you use the telephone.

Tips

- Adding fluctuation to your voice keeps the listener interested. Subtle changes in your voice attract and maintain attention. Review the chapter on vocal image.
- Always place the mouthpiece directly in front of your mouth, never above or below your mouth. Placing the mouthpiece directly over the mouth makes the presence of your voice stronger and prevents ambient background sounds from interfering with your message.
- If you use a telephone headset, make sure the mouthpiece is close enough for a good, strong voice signal.

- Do not get too comfortable in your chair. Sit on the edge of your chair or stand while speaking. This gives you and your voice energy. It will sound more alive and awake. It will also help you think quicker and clearer.
- Give your **full** concentration to a phone call. Do not watch TV, listen to the radio or draft a memo at the same time. It will distract you beyond belief.
- In one-on-one conversations or conference calls, always allow the other person or persons to finish what they are saying before speaking. Two or more people speaking at the same time is only difficult to understand noise.
- Putting a smile on your *face* puts a smile in your *voice*. Do you know how friendly and inviting a smile *sounds*? This is a common device used by radio broadcasters and smart telemarketers.

Follow-up

Improvements I Can Make in This Area:

_____

_____

_____

_____

_____

_____

_____

_____

Action Steps to Take:

_____

_____

_____

_____

_____

_____

_____

_____

Results of Action Steps Taken:

_____

_____

_____

_____

_____

_____

_____

_____

Chapter 29: Visual Aids:

Help The Audience See

Visual aids abide everywhere. They may be photocopied handouts, photographs, charts, graphs, overheads, PowerPoint slides, models, or a rubber chicken. The visual aspect of a presentation is important, whether the visual is you or something you display. Because people believe more of what we see than what we hear, visuals are used to support your words. They add variety to what your audience will be looking at for the next several minutes or hours. They give the audience another tool to remember what you say. They help those who absorb information better with the eye than with the ear.

Tips

- Always practice the use of your visual aids before your presentation.
- Practice your speech with your visual aids.
- Too many visual aids can clutter a presentation.
- Always use color when possible.
- Too much color can clutter a presentation.
- Keep aids simple, displaying no more than three points at once.
- Keep all fonts the same size and style unless changing for emphasis.
- Only show visuals that correspond to what is being said.
- Time the arrival of the aid.
- If holding it up, do not allow it to cover your face.

- When using flip charts or a chalkboard, point with the hand closest to the board. Do not twist or contort your body, or turn your back on your audience.
- Speak to the audience, not the visual aid.
- Do not turn off the house lights to show slides or overheads. You are creating sleeping time.
- Do not read the text of slides word for word.
- Images work better than words on a slide for a visual aid.
- Small visual aids in a large auditorium will not work. They cannot see them in the rear. Use slides in a case like that.
- Give handouts *after* your presentation. Make them listen to you.
- If you must turn off the lights, use more vocal volume and energy.
- Do not leave the slide or overhead up on screen longer than needed.
- Change it frequently.
- Check all machines, have extra light bulbs for machines, check right-side-up slide and transparency position, have an extension cord.

Follow-up

Improvements I Can Make in This Area:

_____

_____

_____

_____

_____

_____

_____

_____

Action Steps to Take:

_____

_____

_____

_____

_____

_____

_____

_____

Results of Action Steps Taken:

_____

_____

_____

_____

_____

_____

_____

_____

Appendix
Audience Focus

By answering the following questions, you will be able to zero-in on the purpose of your presentation with clarity and have greater insight into the relationship between you and the audience. You are not expected to memorize this list, but be aware of as many of the guidelines as you can.

1. Who am I?
2. What is my relationship to this place?
3. Why am I here?
4. What time of day is it?
5. What aspects of the physical environment affect me? (i.e., odor, darkness, cold, etc.)
6. What has been my past contact with this place?
7. What objects are sufficient or of interest to me?
8. Are they pleasing or displeasing?
9. Do I use it or explore it in any way?
10. Who is here with me?
11. Who is expected?
12. What is my relationship to them?
13. What past contacts have we had?
14. What do I know or suspect about them? (either personally or by reputation)
15. How do I relate or feel differently with this audience?
16. What do I expect them to do?
17. What do I think the audience wants from me?
18. What does the audience think of me?

19.   Does the audience know what I want and the extent that I want it?
20.   Am I aware of my impact on the audience?
21.   Does this awareness affect my behavior?
22.   Do I exploit or try to minimize my behavior?
23.   What has just preceded this event and how did it affect me physically?
24.   What has just preceded this event and how did it affect me mentally?
25.   What do I want?
26.   What are my objectives?
27.   What are the obstacles to be overcome?
28.   Are the obstacles within me?
29.   Are the obstacles from the environment?
30.   Are the obstacles from the other people?
31.   Do my objectives or obstacles change?
32.   Do my expectations about getting what I want change?
33.   What discoveries do I make?
34.   How am I changed by what I learn?
35.   Why do I want what I want?
36.   Why must I have it?
37.   What actions do I use to pursue my objective?
38.   What actions do I consider, but reject?
39.   Why do I reject those actions?
40.   What observations do I make to determine if my actions are succeeding?
41.   How do my actions affect my self-esteem or me?
42.   Am I pleased or displeased with myself?
43.   What do I want the audience to think about me?
44.   What do I want the audience to feel about me?
45.   In what ways am I vulnerable to them?
46.   What special aspects of them have generated these feelings and needs?

47.   What special aspects of myself have generated these feelings and needs?

48.   What special aspects of our past together have generated these feelings and needs?

49.   What secrets do I know that they don't?

50.   How adept am I at expressing my thoughts?

51.   What plans do I have for the future?

52.   What do I expect to happen immediately?

53.   What do I expect to happen tomorrow?

54.   What do I expect to happen next week, next month or a year from now?

55.   Do I have a strong emotional life?

56.   Do I have strong stimuli for my emotional life?

57.   What are the stimuli I place my attention on that gives me a true emotional consistency?

58.   What is special about this event?

59.   What is different about this event?

60.   What is urgent about this event?

61.   How do I use my body?

62.   What do I think of my figure?

63.   Is my body used consciously to affect others?

64.   Does my body provide an obstacle, such as pain, fatigue, or infirmities?

65.   How do I use these physical obstacles?

66.   Do I ignore these physical obstacles?

67.   What are some of my habits?

68.   Are any of these habits getting in the way of my performance?

69.   Am I concerned about what I am wearing?

70.   Does my choice of clothing reveal anything about me?

71.   Is it intentional?

72.   Am I comfortable in what I wear?

73.   What aspect of either the people or the environment am I particularly responsive to?

74.   What people do I know whom I can draw upon and observe to use as a model?

75.   Where can I go to find examples of these people?

76.   What choices do I have to make so that my speech and physical behavior is as expressive, varied, and unpredictable as is warranted and logical?

77.   How total is my identification?

78.   Have I used both real as well as imagined experiences?